TABLE OF CONTENT

INTRODUCTION

Twenty first-graders and six teachers were murdered at Sandy Hook Elementary School in Newtown, Connecticut, on December 14, 2012, by a shooter. Sandy Hook has evolved over the past ten years into a key example of how hostile propaganda and bogus conspiracy theories have spread throughout society.

Sandy Hook, one of the most horrific mass shootings in American history, served as the basis for some hurtful and destructive misconceptions. Some people argued it never happened or was manufactured by the federal government as a justification for seizing Americans' firearms, motivated by ideology, greed, or for no good reason at all. They harassed the victims' family members online, in public, and at memorial services, accusing them of fabricating the deaths of their loved ones. Some members of the family have been stalked and made to go into hiding. A gunshot was fired into one parent's house.

Alex Jones's Infowars, a far-right site that broadcast obscene Sandy Hook conspiracy claims to millions of viewers and solicited money for the conspiracy theorists' mission to "prove" the tragedy didn't happen, was present when this horrible crusade was being conceived. The refusal of Facebook, YouTube, and other social media corporations to limit harmful content enabled the conspiracy theorists' inquiries to develop into suspicion, suspicion into requests for more evidence, and anger became a rage when their demands were unmet.

The father of the youngest victim led the Sandy Hook families in their refusal to accept this. The story of their struggle to protect the legacies of their loved ones in the face of dangers to their own life is told in the **Alex Jones legal battle, Sandy Hook massacre**. **Alex Jones Legal Battle** is the definitive book on the Trials of Alex Jones who has been sued in court by the Parents of the 6-year-old victim and features in-depth reporting, narrative storytelling, and personal portraiture.

CHAPTER 1

The court case's legal history with Alex Jones

The complaints against Jones were filed in 2018, and they alleged that the far-right influencer defamed the parents of the victims by labeling the massacre a fabrication and implying that the participants were actors.

In actuality, the shooting in Newtown, Connecticut, which claimed 26 lives, including 20 children, was the bloodiest at an elementary school in US history.

After the shooting, Jones made false accusations numerous times, and they quickly spread among conspiracy theorists.

One of the most vocal conspiracists who spread untrue information about the massacre was Jones, who also had the largest bullhorn.

A conspiracy theorist was imprisoned in 2017 for allegedly sending death threats to the father of the youngest kid murdered in the incident as a result of the conspiracy theory Jones propagated.

Jones's position on the shooting has evolved. He initially described it as a "false flag" incident after it occurred, but in 2015, he made the absurd claim that the entire incident was "created" with actors. In a sworn deposition in 2019, he acknowledged that it was true and claimed that "a type of madness" was what drove him to propagate the lies.

The legal conflict has been turbulent. Jones's Infowars and two other of his businesses filed for bankruptcy earlier this year in what the lawyer for the Sandy Hook parents previously told Insider was a stalling tactic to "postpone the inevitable." After striking an agreement with the plaintiffs in which they agreed to just suit him and one of his companies, Free Speech Systems, which owns Infowars, Jones ultimately decided to withdraw the bankruptcy claim in June.

CHAPTER 2

Conspiracy theorist Alex Jones Trial

For his fraudulent allegations regarding the Sandy Hook shooting, Alex Jones was found guilty of defamation in four court cases. After much delay, Jones is now being tried to determine how much he must compensate the victims' relatives.

Alex Jones, the host of Infowars and proponent of conspiracy theories, is currently being sued for defamation over his erroneous assertions that the 2012 Sandy Hook Elementary School shooting was a "hoax." The far-right activist showed up in court on Tuesday to begin the two-week trial, despite Jones' attorney's earlier statement that he might not due to unspecified "medical concerns."

The amount in monetary damages Jones will pay to the parents of the children who perished in the shooting will be decided by the jury in this lawsuit, which was brought against Jones by the parents. Texas's Travis County District Court is hosting the trial. Last year, Jones was previously convicted guilty in the four different defamation claims that were filed in Connecticut and Texas. Because he failed to turn over the documents and financial data that were required by court orders, the courts made a default decision against him. One judge stated that Jones showed "flagrant bad faith and callous disdain for the obligations of discovery under the rules."

What has occurred thus far in the trial

How much Jones will have to provide the victims' parents is unknown. Neil Heslin and Scarlett Lewis, whose 6-year-old son Jesse Lewis was killed in the shooting, are one pair of parents suing Jones, and their attorney on Tuesday argued to the jury that the commentator ought to pay them $150 million.

As stated by Insider, Jones ran a "huge campaign of misinformation" and "recruited wild fanatics from the edges of the internet who were eager to be as vicious as Mr. Jones needed them to be." Heslin and Lewis were harassed as a result of Jones' remarks, the attorney claimed, which caused them "serious mental distress."

The "most nasty and vile campaign of defamation slander in American history," according to Bankston, was Jones' assertions on Sandy Hook.

Jones, who participated in the trial on Tuesday, left the courtroom during a break and spoke to a group of reporters, calling the proceedings "a kangaroo court," a "political action," and a "witch hunt." As a result, Judge Maya Guerra Gamble warned Jones.

According to a CNN reporter, Gamble reportedly said to Jones, "We're not going to have that again." Every witness, in this case, has been instructed to keep quiet after they leave the courtroom or when the jury is seen.

CHAPTER 3

The Punitive Damages

A jury determined that Infowars' Alex Jones was required to pay two parents whose kid was slain in the Sandy Hook massacre $45.2 million in punitive damages.

Alex Jones, a conspiracy theorist, tries to respond to inquiries regarding his emails posed by Mark Bankston, Neil Heslin, and Scarlett Lewis' attorneys, during the trial that is taking place on Wednesday, August 3, 2022, at the Travis County Courthouse in Austin.
Alex Jones, a conspiracy theorist, testifies in his defense at a trial on Wednesday, August 3, 2022, at the Travis County Courthouse in Austin.

A Texas jury determined on Friday that Infowars creator and host Alex Jones, a far-right conspiracy theorist, must pay $45.2 million in punitive damages to two parents whose son died in the Sandy Hook massacre because of the broadcaster's repeated false claims that the school killing was a "hoax."

Texas has a cap on punitive damages of $750,000 per person.

Parents Neil Heslin and Scarlett Lewis received the funds in Jones' defamation damages trial in Austin, Texas, after the jury on Thursday awarded them a total of $4.1 million in compensatory damages.

The parents of 6-year-old Jesse Lewis, one of the 26 people killed in the 2012 shooting rampage in Newtown, Connecticut, sued Jones and his media outlet, Free Speech Systems, for defamation for Jones' fabrications about the tragedy.

The Texas court and a court in Connecticut had already convicted Jones guilty by default for making false claims that the tragedy, which was the deadliest K–12 school shooting in US history, was a "big hoax" organized by the government with "crisis actors."

Before this, the attorneys for Heslin and Lewis requested the jury to order Jones to pay their clients $150 million as compensation for his "vast campaign of lies," which caused the parents to endure years of persecution and anguish.

Wesley Ball, the plaintiff's attorney, appealed to the jury on Friday to "take him out of this discourse of this disinformation, of this peddling of lies and make sure he can't do it again" by saying that Alex Jones was "patient zero for our society's incapacity to talk without lies."

F. Andino Reynal, the defense counsel for Jones, urged the jury to render a verdict that was "fair and proportionate," or $270,000, on Friday. He had earlier requested that the jury limit compensatory damages to $8.

A forensic economist testified during the punitive damages portion of the trial that Jones and Free Speech Systems, the media firm that runs Infowars and which filed for bankruptcy protection last week, are estimated to have a combined net worth of between $135 million and $270 million.

Jones's net worth was also assessed by forensic economist Bernard Pettingill, who was retained by the plaintiffs to testify, to be between $70 million and $140 million.

Jones "promulgated some hate speech and some disinformation," according to Pettingill's testimony, "but he made a lot of money and he monetized that."

As much of a maverick and an outsider as he is, Pettingill noted, "he is a tremendously successful man."

The first of three trials in which juries will decide how much Jones must pay in damages to the Sandy Hook family was held last week.

Two weeks are predicted for this experiment. Jones will go through two more defamation trials this year to determine the number of damages he must pay the Sandy Hook victims' families. In September, one of the trials will take place in Connecticut and the other in Texas.

CHAPTER 4

The implications of the Alex Jones trial on the development of conspiracy theory

According to Brian Stelter, top media correspondent for CNN, the Texas jury's decision last week to find Alex Jones liable for punitive damages of more than $45 million in a case brought by the parents of Sandy Hook shooting victim Jesse Lewis was a "reckoning that was 10 years in the making."

For the last five years, two Chicago-based podcast hosts have held Jones and his Infowars network accountable. According to Stelter on Reliable Sources Sunday, their program, Knowledge Fight, has more than 700 episodes and employs humor to "cut through ridiculous claims."
Jordan Holmes and Dan Friesen, the hosts, flew to Texas to attend Jones' trial in

person. Watching Scarlett Lewis, the mother of Jesse Lewis, give her evidence and address Jones directly, according to Friesen, was the most moving moment in the courtroom.
Friesen predicted that "almost everyone present" would be affected by it for the rest of their lives.

Since Jones' metamorphosis from an untouchable person to one who is now in grave financial and legal danger, the co-hosts have been covering him.

His substance has effectively been hollow for the entire time, according to Friesen. "I find it much less interesting to watch him now," he said.

Despite Jones' legal difficulties, Holmes claimed that the culture he helped create had grown significantly.

According to Holmes, "conspiracy culture is something that develops through the seams of our regular society."

Holmes asserted that the trial was really about the victims, although their podcast mostly focuses on examining Jones and his strategies.

But this isn't about him, Holmes said. "People would like to focus on Alex as kind of a bombastic persona that we can tease and make fun of.

The podcast format enables the hosts to go into the workings of Jones' actions and the reasons behind these conspiracy theories in addition to Jones as a persona.

Friesen stated, "We approach it with the idea that it's a serious matter. Additionally, we must create something amusing if we want to make it engaging for anyone to listen to.

Friesen describes Jones' program as being "very boring" despite having listened to it for endless hours.

Friesen stated, "I can tolerate that boredom, which is why I do this. He perseveres with the effort so that others can learn more about the phenomena of false information. For them to better comprehend what Alex is doing and what he brings to the table, they should be in a better position.

Many people believe that the current financial and legal risks Jones is facing will serve to reduce the spread of false information and conspiracy culture. Friesen isn't sure it will be a serious blow, though. According to Friesen, "the conspiracy producers and people who engage in the kinds of behavior that Alex does ultimately wind up getting a little savvier." They eventually figure out where the boundaries are between what they are allowed to do and what they can get away with.

CHAPTER 5

Attorneys predict that Alex Jones will receive a sizable portion of the Sandy Hook punitive damages award.

Legal experts told Reuters on Monday 8th of August 2022, that American conspiracy theorist Alex Jones might only be required to pay 10% of the $45.2 million in punitive damages that a Texas jury awarded to the parents of a Sandy Hook victim last week.

After a two-week trial in Austin, Texas, the home of Jones' Infowars radio show and webcast, a jury rendered a decision on punitive damages on Friday and paid the parents $4.1 million in compensatory damages on Thursday.

Jones and his company are each facing three claims, according to Mark Bankston, an attorney for the parents, who told Rcuters by email that the ceiling would be $4.5 million. Bankston said he would contend that the damages cap did not apply but he made no further comment.

The ultimate sum requires judge Maya Guerra Gamble's approval; a ruling is anticipated shortly.

Federico Andino Reynal, Jones' attorney, declared in court on Friday that he will work to get the $45.2 million in punitive damages reduced since it is not under Texas law. He stated that he intends to use the cap, which he confirmed to Reuters on Monday. Reynal reportedly told the New York Times that he anticipates the punitive amount will be lowered to $1.5 million.

Many defamation attorneys expressed their skepticism about the parents' ability to circumvent the cap.

No way are they going to collect it all, according to Texas defamation attorney Chuck Sanders.

If the verdict is substantially reduced, Sanders said that the original figure will still serve as a long-lasting impediment to the dissemination of false information.
The Texas Supreme Court has already held that the ratio of punitive to compensatory damages should rarely exceed four to one, even if the parents can persuade Judge Gamble that the cap should not apply. The jury returned an 11-to-1 verdict in this case.

The Texas justices based their conclusion on a 2003 ruling by the U.S. Supreme Court, which stated that the ratio of punitive to compensatory damages should only rise over one digit in exceptional circumstances.

www.ingramcontent.com/pod-product-compliance
Lightning Source LLC
LaVergne TN
LVHW020546160826
845677LV00015B/4233

* 9 7 9 8 8 4 6 0 4 0 8 8 5 *